The Book of Is!

AN INTRODUCTION TO HOW TO BE GUIDED BY BEING

BITS AND PIECES OF MY SPECULATIONS ON OPTION MYSTICISM

Frank Mosca, PhD

Edited by Wendy Dolber

Published by Dialogues in Self Discovery LLC
PO Box 43161
Montclair, NJ 07043
ISBN:1-934450-09-X
ISBN-978-1-934450-09-3

Also by Frank Mosca

Joywords: An Invitation to Happiness through an Introduction to
the Option Method
The Unbearable Wrongness of Being. Exploring and Getting
Beyond the Myth of Unhappiness
The Option Method Joybuilding Workbook
The Godspeak: A Story of Self Discovery
Birdsongs
The Lightbearers: Volume One: The Hidden Prince
Wake Up to and Don't Be Afraid of Your Happiness Now!

The last unfinished manuscript of Frank Mosca, The Book of IS, is actually more grounded in completeness of thought and prose and shows the reader no poignancy; it stands firm in word with minor volume. Mosca introduces concepts as Dostoevsky introduced characters; there is a bold blending of spiritual warfare amongst word defilades to hurdle. I found myself rereading pages in grin. The lucid wording does not only convey feelings, it teaches the how and shows the flow of freedom to feel. He speaks of meanings, origins and limitations of beliefs in no uncertain terms. He was as dynamic a man in speech or print. Highly recommended.

John Perretti, author, former pugilist and sports commentator

Table of Contents

I. IS!

II. BELIEFS

III. LOVE

IV. QUESTIONS AND ANSWERS

There is no greater gift you can give than your presence among other humans as a totally happy person. However others may seem to struggle with that, they will never have a greater opportunity to make that same happiness real for themselves than being exposed to how that is experienced by another happy being.

So here's to growing kindness and compassion to yourself, each moment insofar as it is real for you.

Best, Frank

Acknowledgments

Thank you, Linda Mosca, for your generosity, trust and patience in allowing me to edit and publish Frank's manuscript. Thank you, John Perretti, for your reading and encouragement. Many thanks to Ira Reid for reading the manuscript and for your wonderful, wonderful poem written with such love. Thank you, Howard Brown, for your gorgeous photos and your never-ending support of me. And thank you to our community of Option students and teachers, who saw the first version of this work. You were Frank's last audience. Enraptured by his luminous words and spirit, you were an inspiration to him to the end.

In the Now

In the now. There is no thought

No beliefs. No myths.

There is no unhappiness

In the now.

No rules. No cages.

No ifs. No buts

In the now.

In the now

There are no judgments.

No dreams. No fantasies.

No past. No memories.

No me. No you.

Just the isness

Of being.

Right now.

In the now.

Ira Reid

Introduction

Frank Mosca was my beloved friend and colleague. I had the joy of working with him for several years in our mutual desire to spread Option Method teachings as created by Bruce Di Marsico. We were both passionate that the essential core and practice of the teaching be preserved because they dive right to the heart of all we need to know about what Frank calls Being/Freedom/Happiness. Frank was the beloved teacher of our Option Method students as well, who will forever remember his joyful wisdom, his laughter and his love for all of us.

Frank wrote many books about The Option Method, but The Book of Is was meant to be the culmination of over 40 years of living, teaching and meditating upon its profound meaning. He didn't finish the book, and I have taken the liberty of rounding it out to some extent with writings that he shared with us, as well as answers to questions that the students posed. I'm not sure where Frank would have taken the book, but in my view, it is perfect as it is. He has captured all that is essential to understand about a method and way of thinking that "offers the light of being, being free and being happy," in Frank's words.

If you love the ideas in this little book and wonder if it is possible to live them, I want you to know that Frank did – in so many ways. It was most apparent in the last two years of his life when ALS swept through his body. Bit by bit it immobilized him physically, but his mind, spirit, joy and happiness continued to soar and reach new heights of knowing and being. I remember him saying to me toward the end that he had never been happier in his life. I knew that to be true from our frequent conversations over the course of his illness. He would bring me up to date on research and therapies, the progress of his physical state and then we would commune about the inexorable surge of happiness, the never-ending freedom we all share to experience a reality free from constraining narratives, our connection with all that is and our amazing potential to live in Being/Freedom/Happiness. I will always cherish those conversations with him.

If Frank could dedicate this book, I think he would dedicate it to all his loved ones – those closest to him and those who inhabit "the family of being" in his words. He would wish that this book would simply remind you of something that you always knew but may have forgotten – that happiness is what we are, what we are always tending toward, what we cherish above all else.

In the spirit of the hummingbird, fly in your freedom, play in the light and enjoy!

Thank you, Frank.

Wendy Dolber

Montclair, NJ

November, 2017

THE BOOK OF IS!

These are my thoughts about Option as the ultimate Philosophy of Being. I begin with the notion of IS as the core conception of that state that binds together the eternal now with the ever evolving now, the unity and oneness of all with the infinitely varied landscape of the many and particular.

Frank Mosca, Summer 2015

I. IS

1 IS!

Is!

The state of absolute potential. The "ghost like" state of pure information in a dimensionless context having no time, weight, direction, velocity, motion of any discernible kind.

IS, IS!

This is the ultimate primordial predication: reality is predicating itself! That predication sets off the exploding cascade of Being, as the indescribable panoply of reality evolving, coming into being in the vast, endless possibility space of Time/Space.

IS is Being when taken as the dynamic evolving reality that constitutes both the universal and the particular of each given moment.

IS is Freedom when understood that our experience of Being follows along exactly with our wanting to know and to know endlessly without restraint of any kind.

IS is Happiness when understood as the ongoing realization of the never-ending potentials of experiencing Being and Freedom.

That began an unfinished book I worked on decades ago. It defines the core of the Option Method. The core of its wisdom. In brief, as long as you allow the basic loop of the specific moment linked with the universal state of being to be the ongoing point of departure for how you engage your existential state, you are on the only solid ground that there is, the only true knowing you can know.

All else are assumptions, imperfect predications about the contingent realm which seems to be ruled by the impersonal, unrelated laws of physics. So the initial conditions of your encounter with yourself are going to shape your experiential destiny. It will form the architecture of your beliefs, be the main resource for the narrative that you unfold from moment to moment.

2 BEING KNOWS NO BOUNDS

In all our narratives, only the linking notion of IS, is indisputable. All other predicates, which are not transforms of IS, can be disputed and disconfirmed or subject to the pangs of doubt! IS is utterly necessary, since all of human discourse (indeed all that is on every level of reality) is an endless series of predicates.

Being is always pregnant with predication. There is nothing stagnant or iconic about being. Indeed the word "nothing" has no meaning except if one is speaking about the apparent state of non-specification, which itself is merely looking at being with one eye closed as it were.

There is only being. The ongoing question: "why is there something rather than nothing?" eternally begs itself. When scientists spoke or speak of anything that would seem to have the quality of nonbeing, it is always proved to be a misapprehension.

Being is bursting with chiralities. Absolutely everything that is, is "tending" in some way. Everything has its gravitational field. The "weight" of its presence bends the light of relatedness to itself or repels it. One can speak of mechanical valences and determined vectors, but at any given instant there is no sum over observation that can capture being in a determined inevitable way.

Being knows no bounds and while "laws" there may be, they are the outcome of an unimaginable synergy of tending and ultimately intending that over eons reveals an astonishing emerging scaffold of architecture beyond any possible conceit.

There is a vast symphony of resonating loops operating on every level. This is an endless layering of fractal self similarity that marks every morsel of reality with an unmistakable kinship! We are one in our eternally evolving manyness. Thus are we never alone or isolated. All within and around us is our relative, our Family of Being.

This points the way to how to proceed as knowing knowers. Our clear path is to sustain and actively engage in the seeding of this process. We birth reality with every predication. The closer we hew to the truth of being, the more we experience the symphonic brilliance of our destinies.

Happiness is the outcome of our acknowledgment of being; freedom is the felt fuel that launches us into awe. This is the metabolism of being, the inhalation and exhalation, the anabolic, the catabolic, the negentropic, the entropic, endlessly altering states while remaining at the core the same generative matrix.

3 IS AND THE FAMILY OF BEING

This is our beginning and our ongoing reality whether we acknowledge it or not in any given moment. Our doubt and denial is but a temporary subterfuge on our journey. It will pass but we shall remain. To be a member of the Family of Being is to be forever included in self similar relatedness.

Nothing is predicated accidentally; nothing is spurious or without relevance or value. All emerges from the dimensionless matrix of information that is both intentional and filled with the wonder of self seeking and creative endless acts of knowing.

Thus, being is the only true knowledge. That is the anchor that allows freedom and happiness to flourish without limit. When predications of any kind are separated from that connection, the path is skewed and outcomes are taken for knowledge, a knowledge without being that is by degrees severely impoverished and creates unnecessary experiences of pain and suffering, as well as behaviors which mirror the fractured disrelatedness of choosing the false isolation of dread over the transcendent immersion in the happiness and freedom of the Family of Being.

Approaches which attempt to correct these misperceptions are valuable to the extent they help a person to reconnect with Primal Awe. As well approaches that are alive to the non-iconic dynamic interplay of self and the Family of Being hold the best potential to be most liberating. Approaches that hold an iconic eidetic like conception of basic reality tend to lose connection with the symphonic dynamical, evolving/emergent nature of reality/being. This is a non-generative static portrait that denies access to the relevant creative reality of the Union of the one and the many in the experience of Being/ Freedom/Happiness.

Also we can do no other than predicate. Our predications can be "facts" as we might understand them, i.e., the sky is blue. Or they may be states, i.e., I am sad. Or we may make impersonal predications, that is where "I" is not the subject making the predication, but rather the subject is some form of "it," i.e. that law is not just. Or you might make a predication with the subject being a person, i.e., you are bad.

As noted earlier, when you move away from acknowledgment of Being/ Freedom/Happiness, your predications will reflect the disconnection. The most frequent result is the confusion/conflation of knowing with believing. All believing is a hypothesis subject to disconfirmation by better information. Whether or not beliefs can be disconfirmed depends on the intensity of the investment one makes in a particular belief, in other words, what you think is at stake. When a belief is a bulwark supporting a purported path to happiness, disconfirmation is difficult.

4 I AM IS UNIVERSAL AND FOREVER

This is where the Option Method comes in, as a means of deconstructing unnecessarily complicated and often illusory detours that claim to lead to happiness. The method is always to question and engage the person in the active unraveling of their own beliefs until they achieve a series of moments when they realize they have no basis for believing what they believe, the golden "I don't know" moment! It is not the exaltation of ignorance, but rather the acknowledgment of having taken as a true knowing of something that which has no real connection with the one true state of knowing, the knowing of being, which is at one and the same time the experience of freedom and happiness!

Most of the value/judgment super structures of cultures are constructed upon a grid work of beliefs that rest "firmly" upon the shifting sands of faulty assumptions; assumptions that actually increase the distance between the person and being, make access to happiness fraught with the barnacles of strictures and constraints of often unimaginable complexity. To exit that dark forest of false pathways, Option offers the light of being, being free and being happy.

"I" followed by the form of IS, i.e.,"am" is the fundamental point of departure. The three statements that are isomorphs of each other are: I am, I am free, I am happy! You can predicate this of others i.e., "you are." "You are free "etc., and that would be true knowing, but it would be predicated out of your experience. The other person would of course have to be in acknowledgment of that knowing in order for there to be an experiential alignment for them. Whether they acknowledge it or not, it still would be a true knowing.

You can predicate items that are neutral. You can say I am a doctor, I am a plumber, I am an American, I am a Russian. These are or could be neutral predications, or they could somehow be fraught with the ravages of the false assumptions of "nonbeing." In any event they are subject to the constraints of your historical context, and the passage of time.

Whereas the simple statement "I am" is universal and forever. There is never a time or circumstance or context where that is not true. And if whatever comes after "am" is the same as "am," then that is universal and always true as well. So, I am free, I am happy is always true. And anything relating to being in that sense would always be true. I am joyous, I am in awe, and so many other statements that are related to being, that are in the Family of Being, will always be true.

But you can also understand that the more distance you place between being and what you are predicating, the more transitory, ephemeral, confusing and possibly the more it makes difficult the access to happiness that all of us desire.

So being and all of its cognates are a little bit like the Buddhist notion of the sound of Om. It is a background, a resonance, a presence that exists always and constantly. It is a "sound" you hear if you are allowing of yourself to be sensitive to it in any moment.

Statements like, "You are bad. I am evil," or "Life is horrible," etc, etc. All of these predications are far from the Family of Being and come forth from the gnarled thicket of beliefs constructed by culture. Some cultures and some personal narratives derived from those cultures are mired so deeply in ways of looking at the world that are associated with Primal Dread and with all the related experiences issuing forth from dread.

So when you look at these two initial conditions, the condition of Primal Awe and the condition of Primal Dread, you get an understanding of all the relationships that derive from those two beginnings.

And the Family of Being is in stark contrast to the pseudo kinship based on Primal Dread. It offers them, draws them to the illusory opposite polarity of being i.e., to nonbeing, the illusory endpoint where the stasis of unhappiness reigns. A place where people are frozen with fear and anxiety, and unable to move; they are in the concrete prison of their own design dedicated to ultimately what might be called again the opposite of Being. Being is motion, life is motion. Flux as the ancient Greek philosopher said is the ground of all things. This next section revisits these themes in similar but hopefully useful ways.

5 FUNDAMENTAL UNITY/MULTIPLICITY

So, again, are all things connected? Yes, that makes sense to me. But what does that entail? What are the implications of that? Problems arise when the concept of the one and the many is prejudiced in favor of either one. It is not the one or the many but the one as many and the many as one in all cases.

My particular concern is happiness and the elucidation of the views of Bruce Di Marsico, creator of the Option Method. My search is for a good way to represent the "initial conditions" of his philosophy. The philosophy itself, the Method, has been explained by Bruce himself in a number of volumes, so I don't seek to repeat what has already been superlatively said. Rather, what I might possibly be able to add is a way of understanding The Option that might be of interest to those who have found it to be of personal value in their lives or of occasional readers who might be curious as to how Bruce's work fits into the larger portrait of human thinking. What follows is simply speculation, speculation based upon my own many years of utilizing and explicating the Option Method and of meditating upon its implications.

A possible point of departure can be found in the objections raised by some to the assertions of the Method. The prime assertion is that unhappiness is not real or actual in an ontological sense. Rather it is a belief, but such a basic and powerful belief that it underlies every human culture and institution to one degree or another. In that sense it to some degree reflects an understanding found in orthodox Christian traditions of original sin. That is, that humans are flawed at the root by virtue of having made a primal decision against the Divine in the Garden of Eden.

Therefore, the progeny of Adam and Eve were banned from Paradise and condemned to evolve/wander the earth bearing this basic, primal fault which acted as a kind of cognitive emotional inevitable added factor coloring and weighting just about every human act. It is an extra kind of gravity that tugs in the direction of the" wrong" decisions about how to live and conduct oneself as a human. Therefore a primal condition of deserved mistrust of self is one of the essential dimensions of the "initial conditions" of being human. The task then is always to be attempting to overcome this fault and return to some state of "innocence."

Thus the notion of being primally flawed at the root is written into the basic code of human experience. While not all cultures share this Christian notion, all cultures do share a sense of the inevitability of human unhappiness. And not only its inevitability, but its appropriateness. Unhappiness then is in a real sense aimed at being a kind of remedy for the primal fault of humans: their rightful mistrust of themselves. Cultures aim in one form or another at overcoming or at taking that basic mistrust into account. In this possibility space it is impossible by definition to do anything else than to tinker with the implications of basic mistrust. Moral systems of greater and lesser degrees of severity are put in place to chasten and constrain this basic chirality in the direction of "wrongness" what I have called the Unbearable Wrongness of Being (eBook by that title available on Amazon.)

So no matter how one struggles and strives, most cultures do not offer any more than paradigms of correction, of approximations of being in a better place, with the constant reminder that any achievement of bliss or complete happiness lies outside this realm and might only be realized in some other, supernatural dimension provided the individual passes the test of dealing with their basic flaw by following the dictates of that culture's remedial moral vision of values and personal/social conduct.

One distinct exception to this general overview can be found in Buddhism. The Buddha overcame the initial conditions of human suffering caused by faulty choices in engaging the self and world by cutting the Gordian knot of apparent intractable human suffering and unhappiness. He declared all reality to be an illusion, the self to be an illusion and therefore all human decisions and strivings to be illusory. The self is the cause of suffering. Here he agrees in this sense with the primary appraisal of other cultures. His solution is to get rid of the self. No self, no suffering.

Of course this raises an obvious paradox, since the only instrument available to the self to achieve its own annihilation is the self itself! And so the self must embark upon a rather rigorous path of asceticism and meditation to disappear like the Cheshire cat in *Alice in Wonderland*. On the way to self annihilation, the Buddha and his historical followers and explicators created a regimen that does encourage kindness, compassion, gratitude and yes, happiness. But personal happiness here is a transient side effect of evolving toward non-self and so still has an ambiguous position in this cultural philosophical system.

The main problem is that Buddhism elevates the ONE and finds the root of misery in the MANY, in all attempts at self differentiation. Reality is not an evolving of endless patterns of differentiation joined by the kinship of self similarity, but rather a formless matrix which is the goal and refuge from the illusory generative realm of maya.

Non-being is the goal, an impossible goal since as noted earlier there is no ONE without the MANY and vice versa. They are transforms of an underlying truth: greater and greater complexity and differentiation is the never-ending fruit of the infinite abundance of IS in its predicative state as BEING! Seeking the "extinction of being" vs. seeking the "combustion of being!" That is the fundamental difference!

6 OPTION METHOD AND THE COMBUSTION OF BEING

Thus, The Method takes a completely different path from all of the above. It endlessly aids one to "seek the combustion of being" (a description authored by the philosopher Merleau Ponty). There is no primal fault or decision that in any way impedes one's experience of happiness/bliss. Why? For the simple reason that happiness is not an acquired quality or reward of some kind for some other way of being that is a necessary precedent or requirement before happiness can be allowed/experienced. There is no top down moral/religious vision that the basic attractor which must be fulfilled so that the occasion of happiness is permissible.

Option starts at the other end. Happiness proceeds from freedom which itself is the fundamental way that Being is manifest as a human individual. The initial condition of what it is like to be human is Freedom/Happiness. There is no fault, deficit, basic mistrust or other qualification or constraint of any kind on that truth. This is the point of departure for all that follows in Bruce's

Option Method. Everything proceeds from this and loops back to it endlessly as the ultimate reference point for all.

So in the one case, you build a vision of what is possible for humans from the notion of a flawed "nature" of sorts. Even if you do not see that in an ideological religious sense, most secular theorists talk of genetic predispositions or constraints of neurological architecture that make happiness either impossible or tenuous. Only with some physical, pharmacological or intense cognitive intervention can there be a partial opening for equanimity.

In any event, unhappiness for these thinkers still is a "natural corrective" a kind of conscience which though formed by culture, serves the purpose of keeping people within social boundaries and thus shapes and contributes to the common good. The individual is either subordinate to the state/culture or a subset of a social system where individual happiness must take a back seat to other socio/political/ideological priorities.

From an Option point of view, a person will manifest the truth of their Freedom/Happiness to the extent that the physical/neurological/cognitive functions of that person do not disallow it. Science will have a range of ongoing opinions about this, but we are talking here about people who are whole and entire sufficient to experience their Freedom/Happiness if they come to know and be allowing of that.

Understood from this perspective, The Option Method shares with Buddhism the notion of an apophatic disaggregation of a kind of knowing/knowledge that is not a real knowing or knowledge but merely a belief or beliefs in what is taken falsely to be the truth. For the Buddhists it is all of reality that is falsely taken to be the truth/real. For Option it is the belief in unhappiness that is falsely taken to be the truth/real.

In that sense, the questioning method has in common with the Socratic approach the deconstruction of a person's false knowing/beliefs. This is a demanding and can be an emotionally intense experience. What one comes to is the realization that you do not in fact know what you claim to know. Indeed what you claim to know is the main impediment to your coming into the full possession of your legacy of Freedom/Happiness. In contrast to the Buddhists whose ultimate goal is to know absolutely "nothing," the Option Method brings you to know one singular and totally liberating thing: your Freedom/Happiness.

So from the understanding that "knowing is being," we see the contrast; the Buddhists seek the solace of non-being, i.e., there is nothing to know; Option offers the fullness of knowing Being/Freedom/Happiness. This is the all encompassing attractor that creates an unlimited possibility space using Freedom/Happiness as its touchstone and organizing principle. All initiatives begin here and all questions refer back to this ontological/existential point of departure.

There is a sense in which the person who successfully employs the Method to jettison the pseudo knowing they adopted from parents, family, culture, then comes to a kind of totally clean palette. The Buddhists call this a kind of Samadhi of being free from illusion, while Option does not give it a definitive name. It is the state of being free and happy. It has no drive or imperative or basic striving in its makeup.

That is the essence of freedom, to be free of all predispositions and a priori mythological instruction. Such a state baffles those who simply read about it as a philosophical description, even as the Buddhist Samadhi holds the same kind of deep cognitive dissonance for the vast majority who are tutored ab ovo in "musts," "shoulds," and what has to be done to be okay and to be the way you are supposed to be.

The power of believing in unhappiness and in a state or states that should or must obtain and in fact do not obtain at least to the degree they should is the prime cause of anxiety and existential distress. The Option Method can be seen as the most efficient instrument, the shortest distance between you and your coming into possession of the full and unrestricted acknowledgement of your Being/Freedom/Happiness.

7 PRIMAL AWE AND KNOWING

As we begin with the premise of primal awe, that we are Being/Freedom/Happiness coming alive as it were in our predications, so we can be guided by what those predications produce.

First, what do they produce inside of us? If we are experiencing happiness in some reasonable abundance, then other dimensions which are outcomes of happiness, or simply happiness experienced in different ways, will manifest in reasonable abundance: gratitude, love, compassion, joyfulness, ongoing well-being, a general attitude of loving dispositions, with special intensities extended to those we choose, a nuanced palette of passions about many things, a general feeling of connectedness to all around us that may manifest as a wide-ranging curiosity about so many things large and small.

It is an attitude of endless knowing, an opening up in our own unique and particular ways to the endlessly faceted dimensions of reality that is a feast prepared to feed and nurture the generations of knowing knowers for eternity.

Knowing is not merely a cognitive process. Rather it encompasses just about every act or engagement one could imagine. In ancient texts knowing was a word used to describe ultimate intimacies. The vision here is not to create a super structure of orthodoxies that would be taken as just a covert set of imperatives about "ways you have to be."

I used the term "reasonable." That is totally relative and not to be taken as establishing again some metric by which to judge yourself and thus creating anxiety about somehow "falling short or therefore not deserving" of being in the elite club of Being/Freedom/ Happiness! You cannot be excluded any more than you can somehow stop being you. You are indelibly registered in the informational pattern that is IS! Your kinship, your membership always is and never is not!

So we are not about describing some "path" of ascension to an "elite" state open only to a few of the "elite" who somehow pass all the "tests" to gain entrance. Not at all. My vision is embodied in the term I used in my book *The Unbearable Wrongness of Being* where I speak of the Great Democracy of Being, where all without exception have equal access to who they are!

The goal here is to expand on Bruce Di Marsico's vision so that one can begin to get a sense of the sublime synergies that are at work as you live moments in acknowledgement and connectedness with Being/Freedom/Happiness, as you experience being part of the flame that ignites and fuels the combustion of being, the evolution of reality, i.e., IS! IS! IS! and from that everything proceeds.

Bruce once asked me what the limits of our presence in the world were. Did who and what we are stop at the edge of our physical bodies? Or are we co-extensive with the entire universe? Is there any place where we are not?

It was a fascinating set of questions and it returns us to the notion of our deep and abiding kinship with all that IS! All that is had to be in some way latent in the informational matrix, the IS, that was the primordial instant of reality. This is the radiance of Primal Awe!

The experience of chance and necessity are artifacts of our limited vision as we negotiate space/time and especially if we move away from Being/Freedom/Happiness
and create our narratives more exclusively from the one-dimensional experience of our engagements with the world, where our ability to control our environment is the result of attempting to gain power over the material world. We quickly discover that this path is fraught with clear constraints of physical dimensionalities that only yield to the probing and inventiveness of technology.

This is an entirely wonderful and exciting piece of our existence and part as well of our freedom to predicate/create/know endlessly. But abiding exclusively in that realm, that possibility space, can seriously skew our perspectives such that we see our destinies, our opportunities for meaning (i.e., happiness) as primarily a function of the degree to which we are successful in controlling the world.

This leads inevitably to comparisons with others where without exception we come up short. There is a play by the French writer Albert Camus called "Caligula" where that reputedly cruel and mentally unstable Roman emperor demands of his subordinates that despite his being the most powerful person in his world that it wasn't enough. He demanded of them that they give him the Moon!

Reliance on the appetite for power over the world always leaves one with the dread of not having enough, not having what we say we need to allow ourselves to be happy! The unease of there being something fundamentally wrong or lacking in us such that somehow we are not powerful enough to fulfill our wants (now of course transformed into "needs" through our fear) ushers in the growing dark shadow of Primal Dread, the potential experience of The Unbearable Wrongness of Being!

8 THE KNOWING KNOWER

So no matter where you are in space/time, in what we describe as history, no matter what level of technological achievement, there will always be the beckoning invitation to know more, to know endlessly. The issue is not the achievement but the incredible opportunity to align oneself with the "tending/intending" of IS as Being.

Every entity that comes into being if only for an instant has the potential to experience its destiny within the great Democracy of Being in accord with its own potentials in that given instant! There are no false starts, no impoverishment of opportunity. We judge things that way rather exclusively from our unidimensional immersion in the physical world where we see immeasurable constraints, challenges, and endless apparent asymmetries of meaningful potentials. A child is born but for an instant and dies. We see it as an incomprehensible tragedy.

I recall Bruce challenging that perception quite robustly as he joyfully shared that to live for an instant or for a century has any actual significance only if we see things through the limited filter of our physical constraints. The moment we move to the perspective of Being/Freedom/Happiness we can see a whole universe of actuality in the meeting of the One and the Particular at a given moment that is pregnant with an unlimited palette of horizons for fulfillment!

Some approaches hold out the promise that the key to controlling the world is somehow to align yourself with the universe (and they give a menu of ways to be to conjure up this alignment) and then the things you want will come your way. So the focus is on gaining mastery over the material world. Very much like the Calvinist Protestant vision of for example the Puritans (which is in some ways embedded in American culture): the way you know you are the chosen of God with entrance to heaven is the degree to which you are successful in life in business and in general.

So the "secret" is a quasi-magical attunement to the hidden rules of the universe which once somehow mastered opens up a cornucopia of conventional successes. Not that there is anything wrong or "bad" about being successful in any way. Indeed utilizing your abilities to negotiate the best situation you can is part of the predication experience.

When it comes out of your freedom to be and be happy it has the marks of that freedom: a sense of freedom to enjoy and engage fully and at the same time a freedom from any anxiety or dread of losing what you may have. This is not to say that the possibilities for transformation, for the "miraculous" are not resident within us. Rather it means that as we may open ourselves up to that, we do so with the complete confidence that whatever the outcome, our happiness is never at stake in any way.

But a much greater "secret" is available to you. It is making yourself available to the wellsprings of who/what you are as a knowing knower going about the joyful opportunities to predicate/create through the instrumentality of the entire spectrum of your specific presence, whatever your wanting might envision in a given instant! The more we approach and sustain our acknowledgement of Being/Freedom/Happiness, the more the sensibilities of our attitude illuminate the true landscape of what IS!

Of course the Option Method is the premier path to achieving and sustaining the comity and presence in the radiance of your own primordial state of Being/Freedom/Happiness. It is precisely a method and a means of initially revealing the truth of who/what you are to yourself. The more you allow yourself access to and immersion in that state, the more what I am saying will emerge as a natural knowingness as obvious as your own self awareness.

Knowing is bliss,
Knowing is without limit or end.

Beliefs are the weeds that choke the flowers
and allow only limited bloom.

9 MOTIVATION AND ETHICS

Motivation is at the heart of what attracts or repels people to or away from one another. What we are always trying to gauge is motivation. We question the motives of others as they do what they do, as they attempt to engage us however they may. We question our own motivations as we engage other people. The motivations of others are important in the most basic sense because we want to know if at a minimum others do not represent a threat to us, that they are indifferent or neutral or more positively, that they are inclined towards us in a friendly manner.

Humans are born into a social context like their primate brethren. Initially that context supplied the fundamental rules of relatedness that determined how we understood the motivations of others. Those who were an integral part of our primordial social grouping could in most general terms be trusted to be either favorably or neutrally inclined towards us. Their motivations were considered as known as covering all cases in this general sense at least.

The motivations of those outside the circle could not be so easily divined. Their group, tribal, collective interests might be inimical to ours. For early humans a stranger was most probably a wild card, one whose motivations and priorities were hidden behind a veil of cultural assumptions that might well be at variance with our own. The old saying about strangers meeting, "homo homini lupus," or man is a wolf to man was a warning to be wary of differences.

Thus from the perspective of IS, predications about self and others could stray far from the fundamentals of Being/Freedom/Happiness. Socrates challenged the young intellectuals of Athens when they refused in essence to grant the mantle of personhood to anyone who was not Athenian. Socrates questioned whether the qualities in other humans were of lesser value than those of Athenians. After a close dialogue they admitted that was not the case. The differences were not in the people as people but in what they believed. So we are back to beliefs. Where are beliefs in relationship to IS?

Dogs and cats will lick and rub against you as a sign of affection and to communicate their own scent to you. That way they in essence join you to them by making who you are a part of who they are, to include you in the intimacy of their very being! Babies will bond with anyone potentially. It is only as they are acculturated that they adopt exclusionary beliefs of their context. So we are born, cradled in the potential to bathe in the light of "IS." Cultures move us away through the demands/beliefs that constitute the mythological instruction that purports to describe the true face of reality.

10 PARSING REALITY

Look at common predications from the perspective of motivations. You are bad! What could that mean in terms of Being/Freedom/Happiness? The answer is that it could have no meaning in those terms. It could only mean something when filtered through the beliefs that serve as the inspiration for such a statement. But you see the problem. IS predicates a state and the only state IS can predicate as knowledge would be a state that was aligned with IS! Words like bad, evil, infidel, barbarian, worthless, and an almost endless string of predications have nothing to do with IS, but are presented as if they in point of fact do reflect an ontological reality, instead of merely a cultural mythological supposition. Only inside the boundaries of that belief system would such predications be presented and affirmed as true knowledge and even translated into imperatives to act. "Evil people must be punished or destroyed!"

Well, you might say, aren't there behaviors which merit opposition and intense passion? Of course! Those who buy into the illusory constructs of false knowledge, of non-being, are responsible for what they do. We do not have to judge them as "evil" because they attribute that state to us and believe themselves to be in possession of a true knowing. On the basis of that they may set out to destroy us. We are perfectly free to thwart their intentions/acts by whatever means we may be able to create. What happens to them is the direct outcome of their following the dictates of their illusions. No judgment of them is necessary as we go about with passion and purpose supporting our own claim to life in Being/Freedom/Happiness.

So you see the outlines of an ethical sense that derives from IS. From a nonjudgmental stance of being totally allowing of all to acknowledge their own Being/Freedom/Happiness, you can see how no imperatives or directives can come from IS that are not supportive of advancing the vast creative momentum of IS and Being/Freedom/Happiness. There simply are no motivations predicative of the true knowledge of being that would stand in the way of any other person's acknowledgment and affirmation of that true acknowledgment.

In the name of what they take as true knowing people savage and destroy others. This is all in the pursuit of happiness, only happiness as seen as achieved only through gaining power and control of others. There no sense of freedom but rather a sense of being driven by imperatives that must be fulfilled if they are to gain admission to some vision of being part of the "elect," of gaining entrance to some vision of paradise, a paradise gained through the suffering, subjugation and destruction of others.

Nowhere in all that is there an alignment, an acknowledgment of the Great Democracy of Being/Freedom/Happiness, of the realm of IS. The Awe, the Elation, the ever-expanding flight of freedom can never birth any motivation to do anything but share the truth of that engagement with IS. What we see in the world today and down through history are the tortured narratives and scripts of humans possessed of Primal Dread. A dread of themselves as irremediably flawed at the root; a dread that drives them into belief states that are in varying degrees the exact opposite of Being/Freedom/Happiness. These are states where fear, anger, envy, hatred, fury of all kinds and vast storms of strife and consternation arise endlessly in the minds and hearts of those possessed of such beliefs.

People often query me coming from a concern that the implications of Option, of the Philosophy of IS, seem to imply that there are no boundaries, no ethical metric to guide our lives. They dread that if they were to allow the engagement with Being/Freedom/Happiness that emerges from the singular act of acknowledgment of that knowing, that they would thereby be disenabled from opposing any action or behavior. If you are happy, then, as they understand it, all behaviors would be "okay." There would be no motivation to question anything.

Of course this comes from a total misunderstanding of the nature of happiness and the nature of motivation, the concept I began this particular discussion with. The basic error is the belief that unhappiness in one form or another is a necessary fundamental motivational factor in all ethical motivation. Unless there is sadness, regret, grief, outrage, anger, or any of the states we associate with responses to human behaviors in a wide variety of contexts, there can be no fuel to fire the required ethical responses to such undesired acts, behaviors.

Thus we see how unhappiness is deeply woven into the fabric of most cultures and cultural assumptions; it is used to knit us together, as we unite to share sadness, grief, outrage. It becomes the banner under which we unite for some common action/response! This is probably the major sticking point for those who get a taste of Option but then walk away, usually in some fear and dread of what they mistakenly perceive as again the implications of having experienced unbridled joy if only for an instant.

They fear the total inappropriateness of such freedom and happiness. They fear it would mark them as being totally a way they should not be. It would bring up, paradoxically, the specter of Primal Dread, the notion that somehow no matter what they do, they are flawed and have an irresistible tendency to be bad or wrong, or ultimately against themselves, i.e., The Unbearable Wrongness of Being.

Now we see exposed the power of the cultural logic of unhappiness. When your knowing is not distorted by cultural assumptions; when you are experiencing your Being/Freedom/Happiness, there is no greater clarity possible than when you are knowing that which is the only actual true knowing!

You immediately understand that in the Great Democracy of Being, all claims to life and happiness are equal! No one has a greater or lesser weight. But cultures are systems that to one degree or other base their claim to relevance precisely on the promise of giving their adepts the ontological advantage of a greater claim to Being than all others! Thus the ease with which the faithful of these cultural/ideological/religious groupings go about destroying others precisely on the basis of the assumption that these people are of lesser worth because they lack the cultural credentials that they (the faithful believers) have. Hence their destruction is warranted when cultural imperatives demand it!

But there is no "inside" or "outside" when you speak of IS! IS is universal and includes absolutely all both latent and actual. There are no special or privileged cases. Your kinship is based on the absolute unity of all of which you are a specific instance.

It is only because the salvation schemes of cultures were fashioned in varying degrees out of dread and the antidote to dread in a universe where Primal Dread is the organizing principle, is Power. And power driven by dread has as its core a basic mistrust of being! Recall the greatest fear is that we are a living unsolvable contradiction. That we could be against ourselves, that we are fundamentally wrong for ourselves. And only by putting distance between ourselves, between the fatally flawed me and the me desperately seeking power to somehow prove that I am not a product of The Unbearable Wrongness of Being; only by doing so can one avoid the unthinkable descent into a hell of a presumably horrific self revelation.

Needing to be a special case derives from the dread that we share a fatal kinship with all other people. Hence the need to construct special cases where only the elect escape the clutches, the murderous gravitational pull toward the gaping maw of the "black hole" of The Unbearable Wrongness of Being!

You can readily see how far these constructs are from IS and Being/Freedom/ Happiness. All their predications emerge from their illusory narratives, their shibboleths and special paths and demands. All their relationships are predicated on exclusivity. Their salvation comes at the expense of others, whose exclusion is taken as a sign of Divine approval of their unique selection. Most importantly, their ethic is based upon those perspectives.

So the motivation and ethical foundation of IS, is its universal "holographic" innate parity. To savage or harm another in any way requires a sense of deficit or lack or need that somehow must be resolved in order for us to be happy. But absolutely nothing is required for us to be happy since happy is who and what we are! There can be no subtraction of Being from itself. Being is by definition whole, integral and entire. We are what we are. That is unequivocal and unalterable. It is not subject to alteration by any kind of human action or behavior. However, we can falsely believe that it can be and that is the tortured path of those who believe the narratives inspired by cultures.

People are doing the best they know how, but that in no way disallows us from countering or avoiding outcomes that would harm us. No judgment is required; no passion fueled by unhappiness of any kind is requisite to thwart the clear and present harmful intentions/actions of another. They are not an object of blame or hatred, but they can be disallowed through reason, restraint or other lawful methods from carrying out their intentions to harm inspired by their blind allegiance to some power mythology of a cultural construct.

Our passionate intensities can be almost infinitely nuanced since there is no struggle to control ourselves since we are not burdened with some forms of unhappiness which are actually clouding our vision and weighting our appraisal with the dark shades of doubt and acrimony. Our clarity is the clarity of being unprejudiced by the demands of culture to exhibit the attributes of righteousness by utilizing the instrumentality of different forms and toxic combinations of unhappiness to artificially skew and bolster our motivation.

No, not at all! We stand in the inextinguishable light of the radiance of being, being equal partners in the fabric of reality. Our motivation is of a piece with what motivates IS! We are knowing knowers inhabiting the very crossroads of the Union of opposites, the symphonic melding of the One and the Many. It is from that place of awe that we can draw our inspiration and operate as best we can to bring about outcomes in the world as consonant with the truth of Being/Freedom/Happiness as we can make them.

11 INFORMATION AND PATTERNS

Information is at the heart of being. I noted earlier that "Is" is a bridge, a creative matrix, the ultimate enabling mechanism of being. What follows "Is" is a predication, an assertion that some pattern or form exists and has some kind of meaning or value to the predicator along a scale of barely minimal to maximally meaningful. Of course, there must be an entity capable of predicting. One could say that all that is, the universe of events, the vast majority of which do not seem intimately connected with a predicator in the way in which we clearly are the originators of predication, seems to lack this point of origin. However, one strong explanation is that an unfathomable point of informational potentials predicated all that is through an "explosion," "combustion" of being eons ago and the predicative act continues endlessly in us and all around us.

The "truth" of the predication is a function of the canniness of the entity making the predication and the actual confluence of the predication with what is. So again we can be accurate or partly accurate (which is usually the case because of our limited knowledge of the evolving state of our time/space possibility context) in pragmatic terms, i.e., we mostly are looking to be just accurate enough for what we want. If we want a pound of butter, we don't require that notion of a "pound" to be accurate down to the level of counting molecules. Some far less demanding measure is good enough for our purposes.

It is also true that we can predicate as real that which is merely a mental/psychological construct and employ it as a pattern/narrative to guide our behaviors and to fuel the expression of our feelings in accord with that narrative. It is the "map/territory" metaphor. By definition, any predication (map) about reality (the evolving time/space universe) is going to be in error because we cannot encompass all that is with our cognitive capabilities. We can be in the position of improving that map endlessly, but always be in deficit in our comprehension.

The difference between that inevitable level of knowledge deficit, which means that our pragmatic manipulation of reality will be limited by our ignorance, and the kind of knowledge we derive from beliefs that guide our ability to experience happiness is precisely that the deficits in the latter impede and constrain our access to happiness, while our pragmatic engagements with reality don't require any such constraints on our equanimity.

We are pattern seeking, pattern making entities. This would accord with the nature of what is, in that all that is, is information and information is the creating of form, pattern, the bringing forth of arrangements that in turn beget further arrangements in a process without end. It is bringing form into a context which in some fashion has form but now is receiving a new variant of form to be thereby further "informed!" These arrangements are patterns, narratives which arise when constituent elements cross thresholds that seem in some sense to await the necessary instant of confluence to be birthed and to birth in a never-ending expression of sometimes known, and as we evolve, unexpected and hitherto unknown configurations with self similar but original qualities. Never-ending continuity and constant and enduring originality weave the fabric of what is.

II. BELIEFS

12 A BRIEF PRIMER ON BELIEFS

The experience of believing is at the heart of what the Method is all about. Remember, the Method exists precisely because beliefs exist, beliefs in all and any forms of unhappiness that is of course. It is what the dialogue is all about. That is why, hypothetically, the happier you are, the less the Method enters into your life as a formality. Bruce set up a "shortcut" to happiness which I cite at the end of my book, *The Unbearable Wrongness of Being*. It goes as follows: What do you want in this very moment? Happiness? Okay, then ask yourself if that is true? Yes. Okay then ask yourself: Do You believe You? Yes. Then you have your happiness right now!

Now that is fine when it is indeed true and that sequence actually aligns for you because that is the truth of you knowing the truth of who and what you are in reality in any given moment, in all given moments of course when understood properly. The sentence that is critical in that sequence, by the way, is the question "Do You believe You?" What you are actually asking is not about what you believe, but what you know. The way to reveal this is to ask it this way: "Do You Know You?"

The shift from believing to knowing is the shift from unhappiness to happiness always. Why? Because happiness is the only occasion when a human can claim knowing and not merely believing. All believing is what we hold tentatively, even when we cling to it with a ferocity and tenacity perhaps unto death. But all believing can be supplanted by information which can immediately reveal to us the defects/deficits in what we are now believing and the unchallengeable (at least as we have to see/understand it of course) superiority of the new information we are receiving/accepting. Conversion experiences can be accounted for in this manner. But conversions can wax and wane as we know, as doubts about the truth of the experience may creep in because other information seems to subvert what we have formerly believed to be something we absolutely knew.

More commonly, changes in belief are much less spectacular. We believed that humans could never build a flying machine. People at the time of Wright wrote long scientific disquisitions on why the mechanics of flight made flight or a machine that flies impossible. (By the way, the actual mechanics of flights are still not understood despite the fact our machines stay in the air. Not to worry; we don't really know why electricity works precisely as it works but the lights still go on.)

In less than a minute or so all that disappeared forever when their machine took off. Or as Bruce was fond of saying, "we all want what we want until we are offered what we perceive to be better." Being offered a check for a million dollars would instantly be supplanted as a want if at just about the same time we were offered a check for ten million dollars. QED (quod erat demonstrandum or "thus it proved") as philosophers and mathematicians are wont to say.

So it would seem that what we believe is subject to rather easy disconfirmation. Well yes certainly when the evidence of our eyes or the quality of what we want is instantly changed by circumstances. If so, then why do beliefs in unhappiness seem so intractable? Okay they are so precisely because the stakes are so high! Now we get into the heart of the issue about beliefs in unhappiness. This also explains why the Option Method can never be logically disconfirmed as well.

What do I mean? Remember all belief systems which include beliefs in unhappiness (there are no exceptions I know of, except for the Buddhist but that is another story) are actually attempts at creating a roadmap to happiness. If that wasn't at the core of how they constructed it, then no one would be buying what they are selling. Bruce noted this, again, many, many times. So if a person is trying to answer that innate tug toward happiness that is alive in every human, and given its absolute fundamental importance to every human, it follows that the investment in a belief system purporting to give an answer to that desire would be enormous.

That truth is resident in the word "belief" itself, which in the Indo European language group is related to "love." Take for instance in German the related word "beliebt" or that which is loved! That is part of the root sense of what belief is all about. What we believe is what we love! Now just try to separate a person from what they love. Okay now you get the picture of the enormity of the task at hand. That is why the world looks and operates the way it does. People love their beliefs, believing that they purport to provide the food to feed what they experience as their deepest need. The truth is that all systems, no matter how well intended to a greater or lesser extent keep their adepts at an unbridgeable (by that system itself) distance from the full fulfillment/acknowledgment of what they so intensely thirst for.

Now you can begin to grasp the incredible genius of Bruce and his Method. It was often almost funny how Bruce would say in the most apparently disingenuous, loving manner, that the good news was that people "merely" believed in unhappiness. That it was "merely" a belief. He of course meant that in two ways (he always meant things in a multiplicity of ways, never in contradiction with one another. Try to do that with anything). The first was with tongue in cheek to sort of "tweak" us and also so as not to make the task at hand seem too daunting. The second, and more fundamental sense, was that it was actually the best possible news. Why? Well, because if the universe were somehow set up so that all there was, was believing and never knowing, then all we would have were defective roadmaps based on ever-changing probabilities and opinions.

The Option Method would just be another such roadmap with the presumed defects and deficits of all the others. We would be awash and afloat in a universe of roadmaps with no possible real sense of what might constitute a portrait of the real terrain, of what actually is the case, ontologically, existentially.

But as Bruce laid out, happiness is not optional. It is not a desideratum among a smorgasbord of desiderata, like a color: option is red, but blue will do in a pinch, or sometimes purple is better, or even gray for a particular day….ad infinitum. It is the ground of being; it is what we are; it is literally that without which we would not exist; there would be no Being. That is why Being/Freedom/Happiness are the same. Just as Being is not "optional" among some other possibilities (i.e., you can only be or not be; there is no other possibility) so happiness is not optional.

Given that as a truth, it becomes the only condition that can be known, not merely believed in. Thus Bruce's happy news that belief in unhappiness (the now understood condition of "non-being" or taking non-being to be Being—take a minute to take that in guys--) can only be a belief, not a reality and happily again therefore subject to disconfirmation. You just have to find a way, the most efficient way possible to aid a person in that acknowledgment. Thus the Method, questions that accomplish the most difficult but fundamental and compassionate task anyone can undertake.

But for the person applying the Method to self and others, it also invites you to understand why exquisite patience and compassion is the desired stance here. Those of you experiencing "resistance" within yourselves are simply experiencing the dread and even rage at the possibility of separating yourself from something you have loved, perhaps all of your life! Surrendering that is the ultimate gift to yourself to be sure, but in the process there may be much kicking and screaming, much fear and suspicion, doubt and dread of what seems to be the unknown. And not merely the unknown but what may have been actually or by implication decreed to be the worst possible case: being happy when happiness has not been allowed and therefore being "illegitimately" happy.

Nothing will get you in trouble more quickly with yourself and your belief system than transgressing against that fundamental law: that acknowledging happiness all on your own, without benefit of clergy or ideological direction, is the royal road to "hell" whatever that might mean in your system. It is stepping in a zone where all the guideposts that you have accepted as real markers of how to proceed in this world, and have what your system defines as "meaning," are gone. Every culture/ideology has as its ultimate weapon the threat of shunning, of separation. The warnings, as you approach what I call "volitional escape velocity" is that you are leaving what you love, what has served you for years, and most to the point you will be all alone with your so called happiness. No one will understand you, much less want to be in your company. You will be an outcast and be swallowed up by The Unbearable Wrongness of Being the way you are not supposed to be (fetching phrase that, what do you think?).

So that is a brief primer in beliefs, what they are, why they are and how they enter in to your personal journey and the journey you might seek to facilitate with others.

13 BELIEFS, FREEDOM AND THE NOW

All beliefs about meaning, i.e., happiness, obscure and interfere with a person's freedom to access their happiness now! Why? Fundamentally because happiness is not a belief, whereas beliefs *about* happiness are beliefs. Happiness is not a state accessed or achieved by believing. It is not an experience you acquire by following some prescriptive path; it is not a trait you add by passing some tests or proving you "deserve" it. No one deserves happiness. It's simply who/what you are.

You do not say "I believe I am!" No, you simply are, there is no belief involved! That you are is the one ground state that is undeniable. Your being is inescapably self-evident.

But you can create all kinds of "as if" narratives about the nature and meaning of your being in this world, most times in concert and collusion with some cultural perspective that encourages and even provides templates for narratives that fit the model of that culture's mythological instruction.

You can insist that there are ways you "should or must" be before you can legitimately lay claim to your happiness. You can construct around this a vast repertoire of stories, narratives designed to buttress your vision of yourself and the world. These can become powerful, what I call, "narrative storms" constructed, woven out of your experience/interpretations of what you call the past. These get whipped up into a frenzy of regrets, dreads, when combined with anticipations of how the ways you have been inevitably define and decree how you will and many times must be in a place called the future, a place that is totally nonexistent, but totally believed to be the only "reality" you can experience.

Thus what gets completely obscured and buried in this whirling tsunami of affective narrative storms is precisely the only actual reality over which you or anyone else has any actual leverage: THE NOW!

All the predications emerging from this condition are judgments that encourage and support the presuppositions resident in the swirling fog and mist of the narratives; these generate endless repetitive loops that reinforce the momentum and agonies of the stories you tell yourself and others. In this context the NOW is never allowed to emerge but rather is presumptively drowned in the giant noise of the narrative. Additionally, the sense of a lack of freedom prevails. The more intense the belief/narrative, the more a sense of being in the grips of its control and compulsion.

If you interrupt the person, you will see a great deal of anxiety or annoyance surface, since immersion in the ocean of the narrative is believed to be the only way to avoid even greater unhappiness. And if the narrative fails, then a possible even more powerful script of depression and desolation may grip the person, i.e., the sense of The Unbearable Wrongness of Being! Hence the power of the narrative as a firewall against greater perceived possible horrors and the intense resistance and sometimes rage when the narrative is challenged in any way.

The Option Method gets around this by questioning the person in a totally non judgmental manner, so as to allay any sense you are threatening their narratives. The questions are designed gently to ascertain what they mean by what they say and thus possibly allowing them to arrive at the "I don't know" moment; this may open up the door to a possible actual encounter with the NOW without the noise and distraction of the narrative clouding the possible truth of what they could come to know in this moment: their happiness NOW!

Thus the deconstruction of the stories we tell ourselves is made possible by a successful dialogue that brings one to this moment. The surrender of the conditioned beliefs about the possibility of happiness and the acknowledgment of our true nature as Being/Freedom/Happiness is the goal and the genius of the Option Method.

14 THE OPTION METHOD INVITATION AND QUESTIONS

[Editor's Note. Although Frank did not include all the model Option Method questions in his manuscript, I have decided to include them here. As Bruce Di Marsico always said: "Have fun with them!"]

From *Unlock Your Happiness with Five Simple Questions* by Bruce M. Di Marsico.

> When you are unhappy, it is because you believe you should be. You feel it is necessary. Whenever you are unhappy (or angry, sad, frightened; use your own words) you can become happy by asking yourself: if it were possible, would I like to be happy and suffer less? If your answer is YES, then ask yourself the Option Method questions:

What am I unhappy [use your word] about?

What do I mean?

What is it about that, that makes me unhappy?

What do I mean?

What am I afraid it would mean if I were not unhappy about that? Or

What am I afraid would happen if I were not unhappy about that?

Why would it have to mean that?

Do I still believe that being happy would be bad for me right now?

15 GETTING BEYOND OUR SELF OPERATING SYSTEM OF BELIEFS

Narrative time is the measure of the ongoing "conversation" you have in your mind/head as you journey through your time/space context. The issue about happiness arises because in narrative time you are already "captured" as it were by the appraisals about yourself and the world that you have made and that are your "SOS" or Self Operating System. This is the repository of your beliefs, dynamically operating instant to instant guiding and directing the arrangement of your thoughts/emotions about whatever presents itself to you in a given moment.

The problem is that you cannot get "outside" the narrative stream, so you cannot modify its momentum and teleology by trying to utilize the narrative to alter the fundamental architecture of that same narrative. You will just loop around endlessly as the narrative constrains and limits your ability to see anything other than the internal landscape that the logic of the narrative permits. This is why people become depressed, frustrated and hopeless! Despite what seems like endless attempts to break out of the ceaselessly repeating patterns of their miseries, they always end up in the same dark dead ends. No wonder the fundamental suspicion that "there must be something fundamentally wrong with me" arises and can permeate our experience with "The Unbearable Wrongness of Being" me state.

This is where Option enters in. The Greeks had several words for time. One was Chronos, or the sense of moving from one moment to the next measured in seconds, hours, months, years. Narrative time flows through the experience of Chronos. Then there was Kairos, or timeless time, or what I call "zero" time. It is blending of the specific and the universal into a blinding flash of awe-filled comprehension. It is that state of being that the Option questions are designed to make available to the person. It is why they are questions and not statements. Statements are declarations about some aspect of reality that a person is defining in some way to be the way that the person declares it to be.

To say "the sky is blue" would probably get you a large percentage of comfortable agreement from most people you encounter. The logic of most narratives would not be threatened by such a statement. But the declaration that "happiness is not just the goal but the actual default state for all humans when properly grasped and acknowledged," such a statement would immediately be challenged intensely by most people's narrative logic. Even when one might feel drawn to the statement, one's narrative would reduce it to at best a nice idea, but experientially irrelevant.

Why irrelevant? Because immediately your narrative would run by you a cluster of instances from the experiential repertoire we call the past to "prove" how your many encounters with many aspects of self and the world have ended in some kind of distress and misery, so that the notion of happiness as a fundamental state would instantly seem absurd, or even a cruel illusion to foist upon suffering humanity.

So statements about reality normally carry little power to persuade. The statement "the sky is blue" will be accepted because a person can simply glance at the sky and confirm it. As well, as just noted, it doesn't usually challenge the logic of the narrative. Only two experiences will affect the narrative. One is a narrative perceived as more powerful, or having the power to affect or change reality usually through the exercise of power over reality. This includes many ideologies, religious, secular where exemplars exist which seem to open a door to meaning.

 Meaning is a word which is always about access to happiness. Most ideologies always have a "path" you have to travel, including ways you have to be to qualify for that access. The "exemplars" are usually a combination of persons and achieved power structures (institutions, states, kingdoms, victories) and accompanying supportive mythologies (racial, religious, apocalyptic, etc.) that appeal to the individual's demand that the answer to their unhappiness must lie in clear and unambiguous success in controlling the world. Their experience with their narratives is that things are not the way they want/need them to be because they lack the power to alter the material circumstances of reality.

Alternative narratives of an ideological nature must demonstrate they possess that missing element of power. Thus the appeal of what we call "extremist" perspectives that are attractive because they both offer a path and a way you have to be to qualify for that access. They demonstrate the willingness and proven ability to control reality and bend it to their will. So even when the price of inclusion is murderous violence, it is only taken as a sign of the authenticity of the path. Thus the way of self constraint and submission is embraced as the key to the paradisiacal, salvific promises of these ideological visions.

This contrasts starkly with the path of freedom exemplified by the Option Method, where no attempt is made to "convince" (a word whose root is to "conquer"). Rather questions consistently put the experience in the hands of the person who may or may not come to the wisdom of "not knowing." Not knowing is the potential tipping point where the suppositions/beliefs that constitute the logic of the person's narrative are revealed for what they are: merely assumptions based on the unexamined notion that because the world they are in operates according to those suppositions, that there is actually a reason, other than the imperative that you follow those suppositions, for believing what you believe.

Parting that curtain of cultural assumptions to glimpse the landscape of freedom that lies beyond can be exhilarating, or alternatively can be experienced with extreme dread.
It is a bit like being dropped into space. You might be terrified that you could not exist in such an environment. But suppose you found that you could. No threat of death from lack of air or exposure to the low temperature of space. Then you would notice that you were floating free of the constraints of gravity.

You could move however you wish. Also there would be no privileged position, no absolute up or down, right or left. You would be free to make these up as it seemed to be advantageous somehow, but that would be your decision. All agency about your "attitude" in space would be yours; you would clearly be the agent of your destiny in that sense. In a very rough way this is a metaphor about your situation in life. You can seek the gravitational control of cultural "bodies" as a means of orienting yourself, of giving you directions about what constitutes "up" or "down," "right" or " left."

Reality offers these options both through the laws of physics and the cultural traditions humans have constructed over time. Thus you can operate in the gravitational field of points of view and information you find useful. At the same time you can revel in the ultimate agency you have over the most important dimension of your existence: your happiness. You can realize that you are a creature who inhabits "zero" time, the time of Being/Freedom/Happiness which are the constitutive elements of what you are. You control your up, your down, your right, your left, in short your entire attitudinal destiny.

The more your point of departure is what I call fundamental awe and not fundamental dread; the more you leaven your narrative with the nutrient of zero time experience, the more your attitudinal freedom will flourish in the narrative of your everyday existence! Your narrative will reflect the freedom of your attitude even when you are wise enough to blend it with the best of those cultural narratives that are available to you in the time you are alive in this particular historical possibility space.

To recap a bit on narratives: the narratives we create based on our experience/appraisals of the moment to moment flow of our lives are an edifice we construct brick by existential brick. Along the way we lose touch with our own agency and so often interpret the construction of our narratives as something imposed upon us. Once agency is perceived as outside ourselves, the narrative then becomes a history of our imprisonment in circumstances beyond our control. We conflate the causal chain of our time/space context with the attitudinal agency that constitutes the core of what/who we are, i.e., Being/Freedom/Happiness.

Deconstruction then by definition is impossible, because we instinctively understand that we cannot alter the causal chain, but only our stance toward what is or has occurred. Still we present ourselves with the impossible task of attaching our emotional destinies, our happiness, to the degree to which we can somehow gain leverage or power over the flow of events ruled by the laws of physics.

Thus any approach that is predicated on entering into the narrative of a person is immediately compromised by the intense torque of that person's core suppositional state. Thus the answer to poverty is to become rich, sickness is health, powerlessness, power. You must gain leverage over the physical constraints of reality and only then will you satisfy your narrative demand to make the world to be the way you say it has to be in order to allow equanimity/happiness.

There is no guarantee that any action we take, no matter how well-informed, will turn out the way we might want it to. So, we can be mistaken because the variants in our evolving existential context are beyond our absolute control. There is only one dimension where that is not true: the ongoing acknowledgement of our Being/Freedom/ Happiness. We can never be wrong or "bad" for ourselves in this fundamental way; however, we may be in error about our appraisals of the complexities of a given moment and our attempts to get what we want by engaging that moment in the way we think best.

III. LOVE

16 NOTES ON LOVE

Love in my system of understanding is a dimension of Being/Freedom/Happiness. In Deutsch's Model, it is a nutrient that is critical for humans. In my opinion, freedom is what would make love a nutrient dense experience. Without freedom love simply becomes a tool of personal/cultural compulsion. It is so often used as an excuse to constrain and coerce others into being ways we say they have to be to merit love! Thus love becomes merely an empty verbal vessel to carry the meaning any person or culture or ideology wishes it to convey.

But does anyone "deserve" love? No! You don't say you "deserve" to be. You do not deserve what you are; you just are what you are. However, you can hide that truth from yourself and thereby "starve" yourself by denying access to the acknowledgment. You can believe as if your love is dependent upon the appraisals and judgments of someone else. It is like believing yourself a beggar while in actuality you are a billionaire. You just don't believe you are and act as if impoverished. You are free to do this. Thus love is what you are, not a quality or capability added to you.

What is the source of love? Ultimately you are! Others can express love, but that is a free act of their happiness. You must acknowledge your own abundance to free yourself to be available to this unlimited resource. Being around those who are fully and nonjudgmentally open to that acknowledgment is of course optimal. But your freedom is the executive path/potential that you must engender to open up the healing nutrition of love and thus flourish in the infinite wellsprings of your Being/Freedom/Happiness. You are really just opening up access to yourself, to who you are!

To be happy is to be totally allowing of the love others engender in themselves. It is the ultimate act of noninterference and encouragement; somewhat like the metaphor of a resonantial field; the more you are immersed in it the greater and more intense the feedback loop. So what might be called pathways of permission are encouraged by the love others bring to the engagement with another, but the allowing of that acknowledgment is ultimately a singular act of the executive capacity of a human to choose along the lines Viktor Frankl described: "Everything can be taken from a man but one thing: the last of the human freedoms—to choose one's attitude in any given set of circumstances, to choose one's own way."

17 WHAT IS LOVE?

From my perspective, as noted in my earlier comments, love is an expression of happiness. It is that dimension of happiness that is the abundance of our own happiness with ourselves; so out of that abundance we are capable of extending to others what I think is the ultimate caring. That is that we place nothing in the way of any individual achieving their happiness. We make no judgments or demands such that the path to happiness would be in any way impeded.

On the face of it that might seem a very passive way of engaging with others, but look a bit closer. Issues arise for humans because of the manner in which they are related to and how that is transformed into a personal narrative which, let's say, adds up to: there must be something wrong with me or I am unlovable or some variant of this. This is communicated primarily through caregivers whose own personal narratives are imbued with some forms of mythological instruction that limit, inhibit or deform their ability to offer a loving, nonjudgmental environment to allow and encourage the acknowledgment and access to the truth of their fundamental ontological status.

What this means, using Buber's language for a moment, is that some portion, a little or a lot, of the engagement will reflect an I-It relationship rather than an I-Thou relationship. Cultures often will require some priority for a privileged group, while excluding others who don't fall into an acceptable category by virtue of religion, race, ideology etc.

Then of course there is the actual nature of a specific caregiver's narrative/belief system which may impoverish any engagements they have so as to contribute to the net impression of an emerging human that they are somehow in serious deficit of a worthiness to be loved.

What I see happening is that love is not a "food" but an ontological condition which is not given or passed from one person to another. Rather the process is one of allowing the self-discovery of the truth of our being. That acknowledgment is occluded, hidden from themselves by the nature of the beliefs resident in the narratives they have adopted, narratives encouraged by the beliefs of caregivers, educators etc., and grounded in the larger culture's mythological instruction to greater and lesser degrees. So the role of others is indeed critical in the sense that the person is subject to the ongoing indoctrination of perhaps both primary and secondary personages. So can we say it is a need?

A need is that which is required for creation or sustaining of some state or condition. It is true without food or adequate shelter human life is not possible. I am not sure that love falls into that category, since many humans exist and live their lives with very constrained versions of love. Again, what is love? It is a state of self-regard/appraisal. People live in a great many versions of self-regard based again on the beliefs narrative derived from culture and the specifics of a person's environmental history. So again there are many gradations of personal self-regard. So perhaps we are talking about optimizing the condition of a person's self-regard.

In my system (The Option Method), love is not something given or communicated to a person like food. A person is not in an actual deficit of love, but only in an apparent deficit. So the task is not the addition of knowledge, but the subtraction of beliefs believed to be true knowledge, but which are merely assumptions accepted as part of the narrative, but which have the net effect of rendering the person in a felt state of deficit. They may actually believe there is something wrong with them and they are unworthy of being loved.

The remedy in my way of understanding this is not to feed the person what they lack, but to aid in the removal of the blocks/beliefs that hold the person in thrall to that false understanding. Think of it this way: if the reason a person cannot see is because I have my hands over their eyes, then what is required in order for them to have sight? If I remove my hands, they simply see! No other action is required. They never lacked the ability to see, but were only artificially blocked from seeing. What was required was not an addition but a letting go.

So it is with love. There is no lack of love; there is only the block of access by the fact of the beliefs that create the as if condition that love is absent. The role of others here is to make abundantly clear that love/happiness is perfectly legitimate for them to experience and by offering a nonjudgmental context to explore their narratives, they can come to see that they are the ones constraining access to love/happiness. The power is in their hands and others can be midwives to their self-liberation through the I-Thou extension of that invitation to acknowledge the love that is a fundamental constituent of who/what they are! So love is not a need in the sense of an actual lack, but a self-imposed condition due to the incorporation of the perspectives of the partisans of the culture they were reared in.

Love is as noted earlier a dimension of happiness. It is an ontological given. Hence it can't be a need in this sense. There is no "need" to be. Being doesn't proceed from need. It simply is. There is no question beyond being. It is a bit like gravity in physics, an unexplained explainer! So the great loving truth is that in what I call the Great Democracy of Being all have equal access to the infinite wellsprings of their Being/Freedom/Happiness whose prime manifestation is what we call love.

18 LOVE AS A CONCEPT

So often we read how secular and religious thinkers alike place love at the center of their philosophical universe, as the highest possible "good" or "state" that one can aspire to/achieve. Now some might say that here we are dealing with a semantic issue and if we sat down together, as say hypothetically with the author of that quote, that we might indeed come to a meeting of the minds about what we all mean by "love." Fair enough and perhaps. But it is worth noting how Option and Bruce, as I recall very clearly, spoke about love. He totally did not want to place love at the center of anything. Why? Because "love" is a word that really explains nothing!

Let's look at how love is utilized. People use the word in laying out their ideological and personal views. But how many millions have been slaughtered under the banner of "love" as we understand it. Enemies of the "people," "infidels" in religious systems have been exterminated all in the service of the "love" of some vision, ideology, version of God. How many times have we read of husbands or wives saying to their spouses how they now are going to kill them because they "love" them so much that they can't stand the notion of the spouse being unfaithful, or in some way being a way they "are not supposed to be?"

Now let's do a little test. Can you conceive or have you ever heard of anyone, say a spouse, saying to another spouse: "I am going to reject you because I am just so happy that I can't stand the notion of your being unfaithful etc." Simply doesn't make any sense does it? It is like trying to square a circle; there is an immediate conflict of concepts such that there can be no sense made of any statement along those lines. Happiness can never be the impetus for rejection or punishment of any kind. Rather, unhappy feelings that they create when they feel their "love" is being betrayed are the real impetus.

So love can be applied in the context of people being happy and in the context of their being unhappy. What could love mean in the context of people being unhappy? For so many it is just another pretext for people to be even more unhappy when what the unhappy person calls "love" is not returned or is betrayed by the actions/words of the one who is supposedly "loved." Thus love in this context is merely wanting something that is turned into a "need" to have it; otherwise one will be unhappy about not getting what one wants. People are drawn to one another for a whole variety of reasons, biological, social, ideological, etc. The word "love" is applied to this "being drawn to another" but so often in the context of believing in unhappiness, and so, as noted, it merely becomes another instrument in the mechanics of that belief.

That is why Bruce Di Marsico said "to love is to be happy." The central point of that statement is that love is nothing in and of itself without happiness. Happiness is the matrix, along with Being and Freedom, that generates everything else, that moves the universe, that allows us to express that truth through our moment to moment existence. Remove happiness and love means absolutely nothing! So love is one way to understand how happiness gets elaborated by the happy person in their engagement with self and others. Thus it is hardly at the center of the universe, but only a facet, a quality of happiness as it is expressed in a whole series of human contexts. So I am all for love as an outcome of the truth of my happiness and am endlessly grateful that by being happy I can enjoy one of its fruits, the experience of "loving" i.e., being happy with another.

IV. QUESTIONS & ANSWERS

19 QUESTIONS AND ANSWERS

If you are happy, why would you change anything about yourself?

First, happiness is a dynamic not a static state or experience. Bruce Di Marsico answered it simply by saying that if you climbed to the top of a mountain and were filled with awe with what you see, you are not somehow frozen into stasis by what you experience. Happiness doesn't disable but enable. There is a natural momentum, a tending that is a dimension of all that IS. There is not a drive or a sense of must or ought or should about it; the word curiosity comes close to it. We explore and move through the world with an open sense of wonder, such that being happy doesn't limit or constrain, but is a constant sense of opening up to a boundless abundance.

There is no necessity but simply the indeterminate possibility of our changing our minds and allowing our curiosity to attract us comfortably. In fact absolutely everywhere you cast your eyes/attention, reality beckons to you, invitingly, not imperatively! It is kaleidoscopic and in fact the happier you are the more the acknowledgment of your Being/Freedom/Happiness amplifies your sensitivity to every nuance of the fabric of what is: the beating of a butterfly's wings, the sound of wind in the tall grass at seaside, the chirping of a bird, the amazing way a hummingbird can stare at you.

You can move through a dense thicket of synesthetic experiences the way notes move through a symphony. Even in what looks like the deepest meditation, there is an evolving dynamic of changing inner intensities. It is not a snapshot but always a journey through unfolding layers. Thus, freedom is at the core of the mystery of the next moment; that moment is always a joyful invitation, not a challenging imperative. A baby explores its environment and moves happily from one thing to another, not because of any unhappiness about a particular object or experience, but because of the total freedom to alter its attention, because nothing is at stake in remaining with or altering the direction of our exploration. So the question is not why would we change but in an expanding universe of potential knowing, what's next?

How can you anticipate a happy future tomorrow with so many unknown potentially detrimental things that could happen?

In this *Book of Is*, the title holds the answer. IS is always only now. Any other time than now is merely a hypothesis. It has no ontological reality because it is not an "actionable" reality. Now and now alone is an "actionable" reality, the only moment that you can acknowledge your Being/Freedom reality. You can of course talk about some other time, and you can be unhappy about such a hypothetical time, but your unhappiness can of course only be now. You can't be either happy or unhappy next week now! You can only experience yourself now.

So while you can of course do what you want to organize reality to bring about what you consider the optimal outcomes, you understand that those efforts are subject to all the almost infinite variables over which you may have limited or no control. Only one dimension remains forever and unchangeable in your hands: the attitude you take toward what is in this moment; only now can you acknowledge your Being/Freedom/ Happiness.

So anticipating unhappiness is simply being unhappy now about some hypothetical narrative or set of circumstances that you are essentially saying must be the way you say they have to be in order for you to allow yourself to be happy!

The question is always unalterably: how do you want to be right now? Would it be okay to be happy even if some hypothetical circumstances were not to be the way you would want them to be? As always the answer rests with you. So what do you say right now as you are reading this?

If I am happy, why would I want to change anything?

One frequent misunderstanding about being happy is that it somehow disempowers you, that to be happy means that you are stuck with all the behaviors of people around you because, well, you are happy so what's the difference! Not at all. Being happy simply means you don't have to judge or blame people, but you can certainly hold them responsible for what they do.

You can act decisively and passionately in response to the actions of others. Our society after all has rules, codes etc. Now we may not find a bunch of them congenial, but even so we may find it convenient and in our interests to conform to those rules. And if there are people in your sphere of work who are acting in ways which by design, intent or in error bring harm or distress to others, you are free to bring to bear the weight of the rules not to blame but to hold responsible and to communicate that you are willing to step in and as best you can monitor the interpersonal environment so that physical violence or attempts to diminish the worth of others will bring the appropriate allowed consequences.

While you may not feel vulnerable to the attitudinal stances of others who may seek to somehow make you unhappy, most will still feel that way, especially young people. Defining the rules of interpersonal engagement is not to judge or blame but to inform all participants of what entering that environment will entail, i. e., a willingness to abide by the rules. So remember it is unhappiness that makes you "stupid" not happiness. Happiness gives the freedom and presence of mind to respond respectfully but decisively when you determine that makes sense.

What do we need to find the truth?

The faculties, mechanisms by which we understand ourselves and the world are the same, whether believing or knowing. We perceive the world, including internal psychological and bodily events and we appraise what we perceive using what we believe or what we know. What we know would only relate to happiness and the core of Being/Freedom/Happiness. Obviously that is central to who/what we are. All the rest of our perceptions of the universe are guesses and estimates, predictions and projections based upon what we think is the best information available at any given time. In this realm, beliefs in point of fact rule the day. We believe about the world what we believe until we come upon what we understand to be better and then we change our beliefs in accordance with this new information.

Happiness is the exception. Here we could come to acknowledge, affirm, know the truth about our happiness. What could ever be better than our happiness? Nothing. All we do we do for happiness so the only issue is what is the most direct method of exposing that truth, acknowledging it and then finding ourselves inhabiting, living, breathing, having our being as free happy creatures.

So there is no disability in letting go of beliefs. The underlying mechanism is the same. In the case of happiness, knowing is the singular achievement of the human being. We are one with what we are through this acknowledgment. All other instances are either false in that they do not in fact get us what we want; most fundamentally they impede our acknowledgment of happiness. Or, they serve us pragmatically as long as they do and we decide about that. We used a dial phone until we adopted cell phones. We adopt new technologies at an ever rapid rate. Some of our beliefs in this sphere may be inaccurate, indeed will be inaccurate because the information that exists is functionally without end.

Well, so what? We move through the world in the most efficient manner as it seems to make sense to us. The truth, the only truth which is of singular importance is acknowledging, living our happiness. All other searches for "truths" involve an endless tweaking of information and so we have relative "truth" that serves until replaced by better relative "truths."

And let's recall that the Option Method is not about putting together an intellectual puzzle. No one has ever been convinced of the truth of their happiness simply by tracing the outlines of the philosophical argument for Option. Rather only in the cauldron of a full experiential coming to know one's happiness is there a true changing of one's mind from believing to knowing. As well, happiness is the reality we seek; no other information however exotic or worthwhile from a pragmatic perspective has to be added to our happiness in order to make it valid.

So knowing happiness leaves no mystery here. Often people will speak of the mystery of happiness but what they really mean is that because things are not the way they should be, i.e., that they believe there is a thing called "mystery" standing in the way, then they can't be happy. So what Bruce brought is a complete dispelling of any mystery surrounding happiness. He was in that sense the supreme realist and rationalist. Option is the dispelling of mystery and the acquisition of the full and real clarity that only knowing can bring.

There are puzzles to the universe to be sure; endless codes and hypotheses, to parse out and perhaps to bring to some pragmatic disposition for us to employ. But this is another domain, one we can play in and engage with open-minded wonder. So enjoy what you know, employ the Method as you will and much joy to all.

How does Option look at wanting, needing and caring?

Let's start with the notion of care or caring. I recall one very intense session where Bruce questioned us closely on our view about caring. The point he was trying to make is that for most people who believe in unhappiness, "caring" is a kind of challenging word. It is so often flung in the face of people as a kind of test of whether they are being the way they are supposed to be or not. So many people dread the challenge: "Are you saying you don't care about that?" "That" being whatever the challenging person believes is the way the challenged person is supposed to be, but seems not to be; thus the question.

It tends to intimidate most people who either will retreat and recant whatever they said or will angrily deny that whatever they said means "they don't somehow care!" If you will listen to the last talk Bruce gave, [available at http://www.dialoguesinselfdiscovery.com/store you will find a moment when as he is explaining the Option questions, he explores the question: "Would it mean anything about you if you were not unhappy about that?" Then he notes that what a lot of people are avoiding at all costs with this question is the possible accusation that if they weren't unhappy it would mean "they don't care." So he raises the question: "suppose you don't care, why would that mean anything about you?" He doesn't say it exactly in that way but that is the core of what he is getting at.

"Caring" for the unhappy, is so often deeply integrated into the cultural systems that rule people's lives. So there is a whole list of things which the "culturally correct" must or ought to care about. To express any kind of view that would indicate to the "culturally correct" that you don't care, will bring the wrath of accusation that you are in some fundamental way lacking in, well, "caring" whatever that might mean in whatever context it might arise. "Caring" and the alleged lack or insufficiency thereof is so often flung back and forth in relationships as the most powerful "thunderbolts" to skewer the other person and demonstrate how far they are from being the way they are supposed to be.

So again "caring" for the unhappy simply becomes another word for the dogma of owing, ought, should, must, have to; a cultural mold that one has to fit into or at least pretend to fit into in order to be seen as acceptable. Caring is simply another word for wanting whatever you want. To say you care is to say you want a particular state or condition to obtain in whatever context that might be. It either will or will not in the same way that you will either get what you want or not.

You may well not want some things to be in any special kind of condition or not, and thus to say you don't care would be accurate in the sense that you want what you want and don't want what you don't want. That other people may find that "wrong" or "unacceptable" or "cold" or "lacking in empathy and human warmth" etc. and etc. is not different from people being unhappy when we do not accept their versions of how we "must" or "ought" or "should" etc. be ways that we have no interest in being.

This brings us to wanting itself. Bruce did not place wanting at the center of Option. The goal of Option was to reveal the truth of happiness to yourself. Bruce was fond of quipping that as far as wanting is concerned: "Well, if God really wants me to want something, then okay I'll want something." Remember the world is set up in such a way that wanting, which is readily and regularly turned into "needing" drives most of people's lives and the societies/cultures they live in. All around us is constructed to create new things to "want/need" and then to pander to those wants/needs.

Every web page is festooned with things to want/need. People can feel as if they are drowning in an ocean, a tsunami of ways to be, gadgets to obtain, experiences to have, all necessary in order to be up with things, to be accepted, to be current, to be part of anything, to have any meaning etc. and etc.

As you grow in your experience of living your happiness, what you will find is that of course you will want things, sometimes passionately, intensely (I like to play at being a big "gadget" guy myself), but at the very same time you will be aware that this is your own symphony, your own creative way you are deciding to be; you are furnishing your world with what seems to fit and changing your mind as you go along. What Option does is make clear that there is no drive, no urgency, no impulses; there is the ever growing comfort of allowing your wanting to emerge from that incomparable state of Being/Freedom/Happiness.

This also addresses values. Most of the "caring/wanting" in the world is wound up with ought's, should's, ways to be which have a distinct moral imperative tone to them. What you then see is this enormous, churning, roiling struggle within and among people to inhabit these imperatives, be the ways they are supposed to be and so often become terribly unhappy when their apparent wanting/needing doesn't succeed and they are thrown back on that unthinkable suspicion that there is something fundamentally wrong with them that they are so lacking and impotent in the wanting/needing, i.e., The Unbearable Wrongness of Being!

Option is the polar opposite. In what I like to at times call that "zero state" of Being/Freedom/Happiness, nothing has to happen; whatever happens is "happiness." Wanting will come in whatever form it emerges from that indescribable comfort. Yes, you will find yourself having values that are often no different from those that others who are unhappy have, except they struggle so often with them whereas your experience is just a natural feeling that they "fit." And yes, you will want things. What kinds of things? Well, read Bruce. His ongoing advice was as follows. "Listen to yourself, be patient. In the best and kindest way just shut up and wait. See what happens. Like a child when a gift emerges, you will be filled with wonder and joy and gratitude for you being you!"

How can I know that what I know about happiness is real?

When it comes to happiness, every other system depends upon some other source for its authority. Some guru, some saint, god, expert whose authority is the basis for you believing whatever you believe. So that source could be exposed as false, illegitimate.

As well, other systems have usually some kind of rituals, values, behaviors, modes of being that are a required part of you being considered as a legitimate adept, member, follower. If you stray from that regime you fall into some version of heresy or fall from grace or you lose access to the kingdom, the secret, whatever that group uses to hold its followers together.

Now Option. You and you alone are the authority. Your experience is the proof. How could you betray or fool yourself? If from this moment on, you were to live your happiness and live it until your last breath and die in that glowing beauty of knowing your happiness; how would that be betraying anything? Who, what, where, under what condition would a life lived knowing your happiness be in contradiction to what it is you most deeply want for yourself? Could it ever be discovered that somehow you "should" have been a Catholic, or a communist or an adept of some Hindu deity, or etc. etc. etc ad infinitum? Do you really think, could you ever conceive that happiness would be found to be a toxic state for humans? That deep depression is actually the only legitimate way to be?

But you, knowing your happiness, living your happiness. This is entirely you. I am not a guru, nor is Wendy nor was Bruce. We are just people totally living in freedom and acknowledging the truth of our happiness. On whose authority? On our own. Just like the god of the Old Testament who responded when asked who he/she was:"I am who I am!"

As I say you take the flag of your own Freedom/Happiness, plant it in the middle of nowhere (which is the unique somewhere of your being) and say without reservation: "I am who I am who I am!" Your last shreds of doubt are the remnants of believing that somehow there is some authority out there that is waiting to catch you declaring your ultimate freedom so it can disconfirm your choice. But there is only you. You and only you can be fully and totally trusted to embrace what is utterly and solely in your hands: your happiness. I invite you to do so, with joy.

What if there's a part of me that always wants to be unhappy?

Let's step back and examine what you say. What do you mean by "part" of yourself? When people talk about themselves as "parts" what they just about always mean is that they are in dread that they are at the root bad for themselves, that they could never trust themselves and so they create a myth as if they were divided (a house divided against itself cannot stand etc.). This sometimes allows them to then say that they can "observe" the other "parts" (usually the "bad" parts) and on the one hand perhaps gain thereby some very temporary relief from having to actually inhabit those "bad parts," but more often it is a perch from which they sit in the audience of "themselves" and watch with helpless horror as their lives play out without "their" actual participation.

So what you present to yourself is what seems like a foolproof conundrum of what I would call "Primal Dread" such that it is absolutely impervious to any intervention by definition. As Bruce would say, you believe and communicate to others that no matter what "even if I were happy and knew my happiness etc." that even then there is this diabolical, so to speak, "part" independent of all other "parts" that would veto, would refuse to ratify what "you" have come to know, i.e., your happiness. Your unhappiness is invincible, cannot be overcome. Hmmmm. Seems pretty bad.

Here is a quote from Bruce that might jumpstart another way of looking at things:

> You never had to be unhappy about anything, but you thought it was a good idea. Whenever you were unhappy

in your life you thought: 'oh that makes sense.' But why
did it make sense? Because being happy was abominable
and that's what we find out when we ask a person what
are they afraid of if they are not unhappy. The answer is:
'that it would be abominable, and by abominable I mean
the worst possible way of existence.' It would mean that
you loved what you hated and you hated what you loved;
that you liked what you didn't like and that you didn't like
what you did like; that you wanted what you didn't want
and that you did not want what you really did want. That it
could mean all that to just not be unhappy!

Okay, back to your original construction: that even if you "knew"
your happiness that somehow that wouldn't mean anything!
Impossible! Knowing is not believing. You could certainly make
out a case that if you were saying that you believed something
about yourself that you could doubt what you believed. Of course
you cannot be in two states of mind at once, however it might
seem so. That is merely an illusion wrought by our space/time
context where we imagine, usually for the sake of practicality,
that time has a continuity, is sort of a block of experience we have
called the past, present, future.

Actually there is only "now." And in any given "now" there can
only be one you, believing what you believe. The next "now" you
can believe something else and so on. To paraphrase Bruce, you
like about things what you like about them and don't like about
things what you don't like about them and you change your mind
as it pleases you. So even if you are now for what you were just
against there is no contradiction. You had your reasons to be for
that and now you have your reasons to be against. Just say the
simple truth and all is clear!

So there is just you, no "parts," just you deciding from moment to
moment what is true for you in that moment. You can make it up
that you are in "parts" and act accordingly thus creating a theater

of dread for yourself. This basic issue is still: what are you afraid would happen, or what might it mean about you if you were not to be believing that? Would you feel ultimately disarmed, vulnerable, finally trapped by some cosmic "gotcha" that is waiting for you to think you are safe before it leaps upon you with diabolical glee to laugh endlessly that you let your guard down. Is Option the ultimate tool of your primal existential enemy to seduce you into a state of complacency? Has that been your experience and by golly you won't let that happen to you again?

Freedom is not your enemy. It is your deepest, truest friend. It is for you to come to know that you stand on the edge of the greatest liberation you could possibly imagine. Again, knowing is not believing. When you know happiness there is no room for doubt or regret. Knowing is that flash of comprehension which lights up absolutely every part of our being. There are no dark corners left to somehow hide a dreaded "part" that lies in wait to deliver a final apocalyptic stroke of annihilation. In a strange way people like yourself are closer to their joy/happiness because they have moved everything down to one existential moment. Change that and all is changed. I/we stand ready to help you. You, the only you that there is, singular and unique in its possible mode and manner of being happy, must decide what will be, what may be in fact right now as you read this.

Is Option a psychotherapy?

It is important as a practical matter to understand that Option is not a therapy as understood in the world of mental health professionals. No attempt is made to do anything like diagnose or treat a "mental illness." No, Option is a method of questions designed to aid people in undoing or letting go of beliefs that block one from allowing the full truth of their Being/Freedom/Happiness to emerge as felt realities in a given moment.

What is the best way to learn The Option Method?

Essential to the Method is the experiential truth of its reality in your life. I found an instant resonance with it but only when I had the actual experience of it coming alive in various contexts did it become more than just an intellectual exercise. Things changed for me that I was utterly convinced could never change. It literally saved my life! That happened decades ago but I never forget that I can write these words now only because I had those experiences, breakthroughs, call them what you will.

You cannot "stage" them; you cannot "conjure" them. These are utterly unique to you and they are you actualizing you! One cannot create them for another precisely because they are not a manipulation of some underlying processes that "take" over and act upon you as a passive object. The Method only brings you to a threshold. Only you can engage your own freedom to cross it. Option is utterly and profoundly respectful of the truth of your freedom. The more you want your happiness, the more you remove your own objections and experience an internal congruence that surpasses mere "convincing" yourself, the closer you come to that threshold.

To convince is rooted in the Latin to conquer. This is not about self conquest. That is the rhetoric of beliefs. It is about the deepest letting go. Bruce often noted that Option practitioners do not push their clients; each question, though passionate at times, is always an invitation. And he noted people will only accept if and when they are ready and we respect that. Nothing is at stake in all this when you properly come to know it.

So my focus at this point in my life is quite different: it is where I am at and I am grateful to have some time to play with my speculations. But at the beginning, remember this is a gentle way; at the same time when you come to that threshold the entire weight of all that holds you together in your present life may present a possible sense of dread. It is for you to move forward. Constant dialogues will prime your motivation, but there is nothing mechanical or purely what people call "intellectual" about what awaits you. Good luck on your journey.

How does forgiveness relate to unhappiness?

To forgiveness! First what does the word mean? Let's break it down. Take the sentence: "I forgive you." Okay, I is the subject, forgive is the transient verb (moves the action in a particular way supposedly defined by the verb to) to the object which is you. What is that it is supposed to communicate to the object? Well, what is normally presupposed is that I, the subject, must have been myself, the object, of some action by you. Said action caused me to be unhappy; that is, I see you as the causal agent of my unhappiness. This makes you to be in the condition of being a way you are not supposed to be.

Right, that is the way the world works. Now if we bring Option into the picture, what could happen? First and most importantly, I, the subject would no longer believe that you, the object, were in any way the causal agent of my unhappiness. So whatever "forgive" might mean it is now emptied of any meaning having to do with unhappiness. Using Option I discovered that I am the one who makes myself unhappy by what I believe, the belief itself being the unhappiness. Additionally, however I might not like the outcomes of what you do, I have come to know that you, like me, are doing in any given moment the very best you know to do. So any blame, meaning here that you are the causal agent of my unhappiness, is gone.

What is left is that you are responsible for the actions you have taken. I am perfectly free without attributing blame or unhappiness to, let's say, have you arrested, if your actions were seen by society to merit this, tried and then sent to jail. I don't have in any way to like what you have done. Indeed going forward if I believe your beliefs are such that you would pose an ongoing danger to me, I might do what I could to be sure you remained in jail as long as possible. In other words I would do what I thought appropriate, again without any unhappiness required, to take care of myself and those I care about.

Alright, then back to the sentence: "I forgive (could be don't forgive as well) you. What have you said? I submit you have said nothing! Whatever you might mean to say is totally communicated in the reality of your being happy. Could you mean for example by saying not forgive, that you continue not to like what the other person has done? Well from the above you can see that this is fine. Still no unhappiness.

Now what the world means by forgive is also fraught with contradictions and paradoxes. To not forgive really means that you say that the other party does not have the right to be happy and should somehow stay miserable for as long as we believe they should. Most times it also means that you retain your unhappiness as a sign and proof to yourself that you are serious about this.

If we assume that a person has been in a state of not being the way they are supposed to be and that results in some problem for you about which you become unhappy, then what does forgive mean? Could you mean that you are now no longer unhappy about it? Okay but what has that to do with the other person? Do you simply want the other person to know you are no longer unhappy about it? Okay so what! Are you granting permission somehow thereby to allow the offending party to stop feeling unhappy themselves about what they have done?

THE BOOK OF IS!

Okay. Maybe they are waiting for you to say this, maybe not. If not, it makes no difference. If yes, then both of you are simply altering some rules and finding permission within the body of your mutual beliefs to feel okay after having felt bad. Culture does this; it controls emotions by saying when and how you can feel unhappy and when and how it is legitimate to stop feeling unhappy.

So forgiveness might just fall into the rubric of a way out for two people to stop feeling bad. Though in fact we know that a person feeling bad about themselves may not at all be available to merely being told it is okay to feel okay. In any event, once you are compassionate enough to acknowledge your happiness, you can see that the concept of forgiveness, which is mired and embedded in all sorts of cultural rules and assumptions, simply has no meaning.

Okay so hint: the best question here is "What am I afraid would happen, or what would it mean about me were I not to be unhappy about this? Fear/dread is at the center of this of course. Fear that not to be unhappy would somehow mean you actually approved of what happened, that you approve of not getting what you say you want. This can easily spiral down to: "There must be something wrong with me for being in the condition of wanting what I say I want and yet acting against what I say I want!" This is the classical definition of being crazy, which is what I call Primal Dread. Hence of course what Bruce said, i.e., that we do not forgive or not forgive because there is nothing to forgive or not forgive.

93

There seems to be so much cruelty in the world right now. Is that related to beliefs as well?

What is demonstrated in contemporary extreme cruelty is the same as always with the logic of power. Power is the manifestation of the logic of belief structures that focus on domination and control of the world as the path to happiness; it is the opposite of Being/Freedom/Happiness.

The logic of power is the demand that the physical world be totally controlled and conform to the constructs of the particular power ideology. If that is in jeopardy, then measures no matter how extreme are necessary to attain the ends of that kind of control.

This is the heart of darkness, The Unbearable Wrongness of Being, what happens when the logic of beliefs takes over fully in the human mind and heart.

20 OTHER OPTION METHOD RESOURCES

The Guru Next Door, A Teacher's Legacy, by Wendy Dolber

The Myth of Unhappiness, The Collected Works of Bruce Di Marsico on The Option Method and Attitude, Volumes 1, 2 and 3

Unlock Your Happiness with Five Simple Questions, by Bruce Di Marsico

Be Happier Now: Your Personal Roadmap to a Life of Joy and Happiness, by Deborah Mendel and Chris Spencer

Bruce Di Marsico Presents the Option Method (CD)

Is Happiness a Choice? The Option Method Philosophy (CD)

All available on Amazon.com and DialoguesinSelfDiscovery.com

For more information about the Option Method, please visit http://www.DialoguesInSelfDiscovery.com and http://choosehappiness.net.

www.ingramcontent.com/pod-product-compliance
Lightning Source LLC
Chambersburg PA
CBHW021208020426
42331CB00003B/267